What Is the Story of Doctor Who?

What Is the Story of Doctor Who?

by Gabriel P. Cooper

illustrated by Gregory Copeland

Penguin Workshop

For M, both my Doctor and companion. Thank you for our adventures in time and space—GPC

For Noah, Joe, and Jill—GC

PENGUIN WORKSHOP
An Imprint of Penguin Random House LLC, New York

Published in 2019 by Penguin Workshop, an imprint of Penguin Random House LLC, New York. PENGUIN and PENGUIN WORKSHOP are trademarks of Penguin Books Ltd. WHO HQ & Design is a registered trademark of Penguin Random House LLC.
Printed in the USA.

BBC, DOCTOR WHO (word marks, logos and devices), TARDIS, DALEKS, CYBERMAN and K-9 (word marks and devices) are trademarks of the British Broadcasting Corporation and are used under license. BBC logo © BBC 1996. Doctor Who logo and insignia © BBC 2018. Thirteenth Doctor images © BBC Studios 2018. Dalek image © BBC/Terry Nation 1963. Cyberman image © BBC/Kit Pedler/Gerry Davis 1966. K-9 image © BBC/Bob Baker/Dave Martin 1977. Licensed by BBC Studios.

Visit us online at www.penguinrandomhouse.com.

Library of Congress Cataloging-in-Publication Data is available upon request.

ISBN 9781524791063 (paperback)   10 9 8 7 6 5 4 3 2 1
ISBN 9781524791070 (library binding)   10 9 8 7 6 5 4 3 2 1

Contents

What Is the Story of Doctor Who? 1

Into the TARDIS 5

Change and Renewal 15

Would You Like a Jelly Baby? 25

The Trouble with Regeneration 36

The End? 46

A New Doctor for a New Age! 57

Wibbly-Wobbly Timey-Wimey 66

The Youngest Yet 78

The One with the Eyebrows 92

Bibliography 106

What Is the Story of Doctor Who?

On November 23, 2013, *Doctor Who* fans around the world had a reason to be excited. Fans, both young and old, gathered together in front of their televisions. Some of these fans wore red bucket-like hats called fezzes; others wore long brown trench coats or vests covered in question marks. It was a historic day for the world's most famous time traveler.

The fiftieth-anniversary episode of *Doctor Who* achieved the Guinness World Record for the largest simultaneous television broadcast ever. The episode, titled "The Day of the Doctor," appeared in movie theaters and on televisions in over ninety countries at exactly the same time;

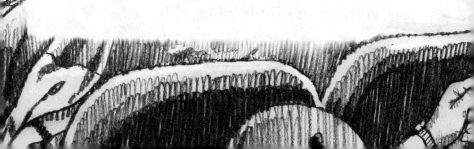

fans all over the world were able to watch it together, so no surprises could be spoiled. A show that started in 1963 with a rather small audience in the United Kingdom was now being watched by over ten million devoted fans.

The Eleventh Doctor, played by Matt Smith, was joined by the previous Tenth Doctor, played by David Tennant, in an adventure unlike anything viewers had experienced before. For years the writer of the show, Steven Moffat, had been teasing audiences with references to a legendary Time War. And now the time for teasing had come to an end. "The Day of the Doctor" revealed details about the Time War and introduced a new Doctor known only as the War Doctor, played by British actor John Hurt. In little over an hour, fans were treated to characters and references from fifty years of the show's history and a brief peek at the future Twelfth Doctor.

The fiftieth-anniversary episode was a huge

John Hurt as the War Doctor

success. After 806 episodes, *Doctor Who* was still very much in demand. This time traveler with two hearts had once again shown that he wasn't going away anytime soon. With fans as old as the show itself, and new fans growing up and experiencing the magic for the first time, the Doctor has proved to be a hero for all of time and space.

CHAPTER 1
Into the TARDIS

In March 1963, Donald Baverstock, the chief of programs for the British Broadcasting Corporation (BBC), noticed a gap in the Saturday evening television schedule. Baverstock was looking for a new show to fill the empty time slot between a popular sports program and an equally popular teen show. He wanted a show filled with adventure that both young and old audiences would be able to enjoy together.

Sydney Newman, the BBC's head of drama, was chosen to develop the show. He wanted it to be educational for children. Donald Wilson, the head of script development, wanted it to be about time travel. The two ideas worked well together.

The show could travel into the past to view important historical events and to other worlds where scientific ideas could be explored.

Sydney wanted to make it clear that even though the show featured science fiction elements, it was not a science fiction show; it was an educational program. The time machine, able to travel through time *and* space, would look like a blue police box. Nothing flashy or expensive. It was called the TARDIS, meaning "Time and Relative Dimension in Space."

Police Boxes

While often associated with the United Kingdom, the first police box was built in Albany, New York, in 1877. Police boxes were not introduced in the United Kingdom until the early 1920s. Most were painted blue and housed telephones for use by the police or by others in case of an emergency. They are different from the red phone booths—also called boxes—that can be found in the United Kingdom.

The phone is not located on the inside like in a normal phone booth. Instead it is located within a small panel on the *outside*. The inside of the police box can be used as a miniature police station if needed. Police officers used them to take breaks, eat lunch, and even temporarily hold prisoners. The boxes stand around nine feet tall and feature two small windows on each side, a light on top, and a sign that reads: "Police Telephone. Free for use of public. Advice & assistance obtainable immediately. Officers & cars respond to all calls. Pull to open."

With the invention of modern cell phones and radios, most (if not all) police boxes are no longer in use.

Scriptwriter C. E. Webber suggested the lead character be a scientist and that two schoolteachers should be involved as well. Sydney Newman wanted a kid in the show who would "get into trouble" and "make mistakes." The scientist, called the Doctor, would remain something of a mystery throughout the show. The Doctor was not, in fact, a doctor at all but an alien time traveler from another planet.

Jacqueline Hill and William Russell were cast as schoolteachers, named Barbara Wright (a history teacher) and Ian Chesterton (a science teacher),

respectively. Carole Ann Ford played the young student Susan, who was also the Doctor's granddaughter. William Hartnell was cast to play the curious alien Doctor.

Time Travel

The concept of using a machine to
time travel was popularized in H. G.
Wells's 1895 novel *The Time Machine*.
In this famous story, the Time Traveller
visits our world in AD 802,701 with the help of an
invention that Wells called a "time machine."

Ever since time travel was introduced into the
public's imagination, people have wondered if it will
ever be possible. Famous scientists like Carl Sagan
and Stephen Hawking have studied the possibilities.
Hawking did not believe it was even possible. If it
were, where are all of the time-traveling tourists
from the future? Sagan disagreed, proposing that
maybe there are time travelers all around us and we
just don't notice them.

The idea of time travel has continued to remain
popular in modern science fiction and fantasy.

The filming of *Doctor Who* began in September 1963 under the watchful eye of producer Verity Lambert. Verity was the first female producer at the BBC and the youngest at only twenty-seven years old. Waris Hussein, only twenty-four at the time, was the director. After the first episode was shown to Sydney Newman, he made them reshoot the entire thing! Sydney felt that something just wasn't working.

The very first episode, titled "An Unearthly Child," was shown in the United Kingdom on November 23, 1963 to only 4.4 million viewers. The episode reran the following week, but this time over 6 million viewers tuned in. The decision to air the episode again had been a smart one!

The first four episodes together told one larger story, called "10,000 BC," and took the schoolteachers, Susan, and the Doctor on an adventure in prehistoric times. With flashy effects, crazy cavemen, and danger around every corner, the show was a huge success. Before long, *Doctor Who* would become much more than its creators had ever intended.

William Hartnell as the First Doctor

Against Sydney Newman's wish for no "bug-eyed monsters," the follow-up story was called "The Daleks." In it, the terrifying half-creature, half-machine villains known as the Daleks were introduced. They are determined to exterminate all other life. After their debut, "Dalekmania" spread across the United Kingdom. The Daleks were almost more popular than the Doctor himself.

Doctor Who (as he was sometimes called in the early days of the show) and his enemies, the Daleks, were now household names, and no one knew what to expect next!

CHAPTER 2
Change and Renewal

After appearing as the Doctor from 1963 to 1966, William Hartnell left the show. How could you have *Doctor Who* without the Doctor? Script editor Gerry Davis had an idea. Since the Doctor was an alien who didn't have to play by human rules, he wanted to write the show so that the Doctor could "die" and then return with a new face and body. The writers called the process "regeneration." It would allow the Doctor to be played by different actors for as long as the show was on television.

Gerry Davis

Regeneration became a big part of the *Doctor*

Who story going forward. The writers decided that the Doctor was from a race of aliens called Time Lords. Each Time Lord, from the planet Gallifrey, is given twelve regenerations throughout his or her long life. When Time Lords die, they simply regenerate with a new body and a slightly different personality.

Because episodes that took place in the future or on distant planets were attracting more viewers, the show's creators decided that they would stop making episodes that happen in the past. Christopher "Kit" Pedler, a research scientist at the University of London, was hired to bring realistic scientific ideas to the show. Together with writer Gerry Davis, he created the Doctor's newest foes, the Cybermen. Cybermen want to live forever by turning themselves into robots. From a future where technology has taken over human bodies, the Cybermen became the first monsters to rival the popularity of the Daleks.

In October 1966, William Hartnell appeared as the Doctor for the last time in an episode called "The Tenth Planet." After defeating the Cybermen at the South Pole, the First Doctor, old and tired, regenerated. Played by Patrick Troughton, the Second Doctor brought a new energy to the show. And a new character was introduced who would become a longtime friend of the Doctor—Brigadier Alistair Lethbridge-Stewart. The Brigadier, played by Nicholas Courtney, was the leader of UNIT (United Nations Intelligence Taskforce), a military organization specializing in alien invasions. Audiences were also introduced to new enemies such as the Great Intelligence and the ancient Ice Warriors.

Brigadier Alistair Lethbridge-Stewart and Patrick Troughton as the Second Doctor

Sonic Screwdrivers

The Doctor's sonic screwdriver was first introduced in the Second Doctor's 1968 story "Fury from the Deep." It's been used by almost every version of the Doctor since.

The sonic screwdriver isn't really a screwdriver at all. While it may share a similar shape, the sonic screwdriver is very advanced Time Lord technology. It has many different uses and seems to solve almost every problem for the Doctor—just point the

screwdriver at an obstacle, and it can be overcome. Emitting a strange whirring noise, the sonic screwdriver can open doors, fix broken technology, and start vehicles without a key. Its only weakness? It can't be used on anything made of wood.

After he had appeared in 119 episodes from 1966 to 1969, Patrick Troughton decided to leave the show. During an episode called "The War Games," the Doctor was put on trial on Gallifrey by his fellow Time Lords. He had been interfering with other worlds for far too long. He was sentenced to live on Earth, and he would be forced to regenerate—leaving him with a new appearance in a new home.

Jon Pertwee as the Third Doctor

The next series began in 1970. Jon Pertwee entered the show as a new kind of Doctor for a new decade. The Third Doctor was very different from those who had come before him. No longer *traveling* with teachers or youngsters in his

TARDIS, the Doctor instead worked alongside UNIT as a scientific adviser. He chased down alien threats in his new yellow car—and for the first time, color mattered. *Doctor Who* was no longer being filmed in black and white!

It seemed that more adults than children were watching *Doctor Who*. The show became more action packed and suspenseful. Soon the Doctor was introduced to a new enemy—his nemesis, the Master. (*Nemesis* is another word for rival or opponent.) Played by Roger Delgado, the Master was a Time Lord like the Doctor, but he wasn't on Earth to save the day. He was there to cause chaos. Eventually the Third Doctor was free to leave Earth once more and travel among the stars.

Hero and Nemesis

Many great heroes have an equally powerful villain who challenges them and pushes them to their very limits. While a hero may have many foes, usually there is one who stands out above all others. This character is known as the hero's nemesis, or archenemy.

In *Doctor Who*, the Master is the Doctor's nemesis. They're both Time Lords. They're both very intelligent. And they're both very confident. Being so similar makes them perfect enemies.

The different faces of the Master

Throughout the series, the Doctor's travel buddies are usually known as "companions." They are the Doctor's friends on many journeys through time and space. By the end of his run as the famous time traveler, the Third Doctor had met one of his most important companions—Sarah Jane Smith. Introduced in "The Time Warrior," Sarah Jane was a strong, confident young journalist and quickly became close friends with the Doctor. She would continue to appear in the show for many years.

Sarah Jane Smith

CHAPTER 3
Would You Like a Jelly Baby?

At the end of the eleventh season of *Doctor Who*, Jon Pertwee decided to leave the role of the Doctor. He had appeared in 128 episodes, and "Planet of the Spiders" in 1974 would be his last.

After a battle on the planet Metebelis Three, a world ruled by giant spiders, the Doctor is greatly weakened by an explosion that destroys the leader of the spider world, who is known as the Great One. Returning to Earth in the TARDIS three weeks later, the Third Doctor regenerates into the Fourth Doctor right in front of the Brigadier and Sarah Jane.

At the age of forty, actor Tom Baker's life changed when he took on the title role in *Doctor Who*. Wearing a long colorful scarf and a wide-brimmed hat, this version of the beloved Time Lord was far more "alien" than those who had come before. He was wild and funny and enjoyed gummy candies called Jelly Babies, which he kept in his coat pocket at all times.

Tom Baker as the Fourth Doctor

Jelly Babies

The Second Doctor was the first to enjoy these famous candies in the *Doctor Who* series. But it would be the Fourth Doctor who would become best known for his love of Jelly Babies.

These gummy candies first appeared in England in 1885 under a different name but became popular and widely available in 1918 through the British candy company Bassett's. They got the name "Jelly Babies" in 1953 because they are shaped like small children. They come in several different colors and flavors: red (strawberry), pink (raspberry), green (lime), yellow (lemon), purple (blackcurrant), and orange, which tastes like an orange.

Jelly Babies are not as popular or easily available in the United States, where gummy bears are more common and similar in taste.

First appearing regularly in the 1974 episode "Robot," the Fourth Doctor eventually abandoned his position at UNIT and returned to traveling through time and space. With Sarah Jane Smith by his side, the Doctor is called on by the Time Lords to stop the creation of the Daleks. They are transported to the planet of Skaro, where a war had turned the planet into a wasteland.

Viewed by over ten million fans, "Genesis of the Daleks" revealed the origin story of the Daleks and introduced their creator, the half-man, half-machine Davros. In one memorable scene, the Doctor is tasked with setting off an explosion that would guarantee that no Dalek would survive into the future. He hesitates, questioning whether

he has the right to make such a decision about his most feared enemies. At the last moment, he chooses not to destroy the Daleks—a shining example of the Doctor's goodness and decency. "Genesis of the Daleks" is one of the Fourth Doctor's most popular stories.

The Doctor with Davros, the creator of the Daleks

Over the next seven years, the Fourth Doctor met and traveled with many memorable companions. After the Doctor and Sarah Jane Smith parted ways, the Doctor met Leela, a member of an alien warrior tribe. They traveled throughout history before they eventually met K-9, a robot dog, who returned with them to Gallifrey. Once back on Gallifrey, the Doctor proclaimed himself president.

Leela and K-9

Throughout his time on the show, Tom Baker's Fourth Doctor made new friends and encountered countless enemies: shapeshifting Zygons, new and improved Cybermen, and the Master, who himself had recently regenerated!

Zygons

In over 170 episodes, Tom Baker ushered in a new age for *Doctor Who*. Audiences loved the funny, unpredictable Doctor and his new and interesting adventures. In a poll taken by the BBC during the fiftieth-anniversary year of *Doctor Who*, the Fourth Doctor was voted as the number one most popular Doctor.

DW NEWS

Best of 'Doctor Who' 50th Anniversary Poll: Top 5 Doctors 4th Doctor voted most popular.

Tom Baker, who starred as the wild and funny 'Doctor Who' in the BBC series that has been running since 1963. Mr...

CHAPTER 4
The Trouble with Regeneration

Tom Baker left *Doctor Who* after the eighteenth season. He would be a hard Doctor to follow. Fortunately, actor Peter Davison was up to the task. Davison had grown up watching the show nearly twenty years earlier, starting with the very first episode! Davison stepped into the role of the Fifth Doctor at the age of twenty-nine.

Some people thought that he was too young to be the famous Time Lord. But if he was a shape-shifting alien, why wouldn't he be able to look quite young? He was already well known by British audiences for his performance in another television show called *All Creatures Great and Small*, where he played another kind of doctor—a veterinarian.

Cast of *All Creatures Great and Small*

At the beginning of the nineteenth season, the Fifth Doctor appeared in his first full episode, "Castrovalva." Unlike the Fourth Doctor, who was very odd, the Fifth Doctor was more human in his actions. He wasn't always as sure or as confident as the Doctors who had come before him.

Wearing a cricket uniform with a stalk of celery pinned to his lapel, the Doctor continued traveling through time and space with his companions, Tegan, Nyssa, and Adric. (Cricket is a British game played with a ball and bat.)

Peter Davison as the Fifth Doctor

The nineteenth season was a big success for *Doctor Who*—ratings had doubled! During his three seasons on the show, the Fifth Doctor briefly traveled with a shape-shifting robot named Kamelion and battled old enemies such as the Silurians and the Sea Devils. For the twentieth

Kamelion

anniversary of the show, an episode titled "The Five Doctors" brought together all five versions of the character.

After appearing in sixty-nine episodes of *Doctor Who*, Peter Davison decided not to return to the show. His travel companion Tegan left the TARDIS in the episode "Resurrection of the Daleks," and a new friend, an American named Peri, was introduced in the Fifth Doctor's final episodes in

1984. The Doctor and Peri had both been poisoned and with only one antidote available, the Doctor heroically sacrificed his life to save Peri's.

Colin Baker was next to play the Doctor. Baker became the first actor to play the Doctor after having already appeared on the show. He once had a small role as a guard named Maxil.

A lifelong fan of science fiction, Baker was eager to bring something new to the character. Starting in March 1984, his Doctor wore brightly colored clothes that didn't match at all! His appearance reflected the colorful fashion trends of the 1980s—a long polka-dotted tie, yellow pants, and a shirt with question marks on the collar.

Audiences were not sure what to think of the new Doctor. At the end of the episode titled "The Twin Dilemma," the Sixth Doctor tells his companion (and, surely, the audience), "Whatever else happens, I am the Doctor—whether you like it or not."

Colin Baker as the Sixth Doctor

In the 1980s, science fiction shows were becoming very popular on TV in the United States. The BBC couldn't afford to compete with the big budgets of American sci-fi shows like *Star Trek*. *Doctor Who* was beginning to fall behind the times.

When TV executive Michael Grade took over BBC One in 1984, he decided that the show would take an eighteen-month break. After only

thirty-one episodes, Colin Baker did not even appear in his regeneration scene as all other Doctors had.

When *Doctor Who* took a break between the twenty-second and twenty-third seasons, a *Doctor Who* radio serial was released, starting on July 25 and ending on August 8, 1985. Each of the six episodes was ten minutes long and featured the voices of Colin Baker as the Sixth Doctor and Nicola Bryant as Peri Brown.

Radio Serials

Radio serials (also known as radio dramas) are dramatic performances, similar to plays, broadcast over the radio. While there is nothing to see, these "shows" feature actors, music, and sound effects combined to tell exciting stories. They were first produced in the 1920s and were very popular for decades. Both adults and children would tune in to their favorite stations to hear popular radio plays like *The Shadow*, *The Twilight Zone*, and *The Green Hornet*.

With the invention of television in the 1950s, radio dramas became less popular, but they are still recorded and broadcast today!

Big Finish, a British company specializing in digital audio plays, began releasing regular *Doctor Who* audio dramas in 1999. Since then, they've produced stories featuring the original voices of the Fourth, Fifth, Sixth, Seventh, Eighth, Tenth, and War Doctors! The original actors continue to record new adventures featuring their version of the character.

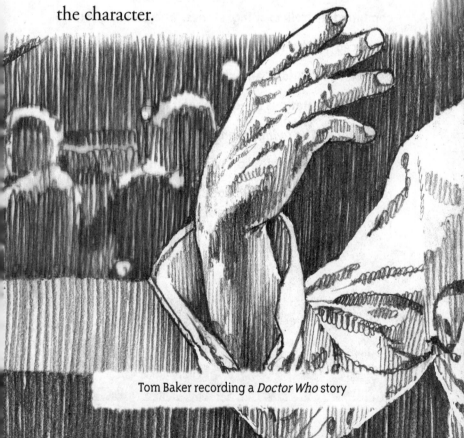

Tom Baker recording a *Doctor Who* story

CHAPTER 5
The End?

After the shortest season they had ever filmed, Michael Grade decided to make some changes. Sylvester McCoy was cast to play the Doctor in what could have been the final season. He was a popular actor who drew inspiration for his version of the Doctor from Charlie Chaplin, the famous silent film star. McCoy brought the Seventh Doctor and his question-mark-covered vest to

Sylvester McCoy as the Seventh Doctor

the series in 1987. He started out as a goofy and awkward Doctor but eventually became much more serious and determined.

The Seventh Doctor carried an umbrella with a question mark handle. One of his companions was a rebellious space station waitress named Ace. In the episode "Dragonfire," a villain's face was melted off! Even though the show was becoming more violent, fans continued to tune in weekly. And Ace was becoming a fan-favorite character.

Audiences were reacting well to the Seventh Doctor. And in the twenty-sixth season, both the retired Brigadier Lethbridge-Stewart and UNIT returned to the show. Fans were delighted.

Whovians

Doctor Who has a very dedicated fan base—one of the largest in the entire world! These passionate viewers are known by some as "Whovians." The term was first used during the 1980s, when the Doctor Who Fan Club of America released the first issue of its newsletter, titled the *Whovian Times*.

Before the American fan club existed, Britain had its own fan club called the Doctor Who Appreciation Society, which was founded in the late 1970s. Other

Doctor Who fan clubs can be found all over the world, including in Australia, Canada, New Zealand, and many other countries.

Doctor Who is loved by millions of Whovians, who eagerly look forward to each new adventure. When they're not rewatching, rereading, or relistening to old adventures of the Doctor, Whovians gather at large conventions. They dress up as their favorite show characters, meet their favorite actors, and buy *Doctor Who* T-shirts, chess sets, blankets, alarm clocks, jewelry, action figures, and even sonic screwdrivers!

Even with renewed interest in the latest season, *Doctor Who* simply couldn't keep up with its competition. *Star Trek: The Next Generation* debuted in 1987. It was full of fantastic special

effects and terrifying new monsters. *Doctor Who* was beginning to look a bit old-fashioned in comparison. In 1989, it was announced that the Doctor and Ace would not be returning for another season. The last story, "Survival," ended on December 6. It seemed as if the Doctor could travel through time but couldn't make it to the 1990s.

Steven Spielberg's production company, Amblin Entertainment, attempted to spark new

interest in the *Doctor Who* series by making a movie. It was not shown until May 1996—nearly seven years after the TV show had ended! The made-for-TV movie was simply called *Doctor Who*.

Sylvester McCoy's Seventh Doctor returns briefly at the beginning of the movie as his TARDIS crash-lands in San Francisco, where he is caught in the middle of a gunfight between gang members.

When he wakes up in a hospital, he has regenerated. Played by Paul McGann, the Eighth Doctor had long hair and wore clothes from the early part of the twentieth century. The new Doctor meets Dr. Grace Holloway, a heart doctor, and takes her onto the TARDIS for a thrilling adventure.

With Grace by his side, the Doctor battles a recently regenerated version of the Master, played by American actor Eric Roberts. The Master is attempting to steal the Doctor's remaining lives. Not only are we introduced to a new Doctor and a new Master, but the TARDIS has also changed. Unlike the previous TARDIS, the inside of the Eighth Doctor's time machine is darker.

Paul McGann as the Eighth Doctor

The Changing TARDIS

Every once in a while, the Doctor changes appearance, sonic screwdriver, and outfit. Not only does the Doctor go through constant change, but the TARDIS does as well.

The interiors of the First Doctor's and the Second Doctor's TARDIS looked pretty much the same. But after the Third Doctor was introduced, the TARDIS began to change with each new season. The shape of the central control panels remained, but different buttons were added or removed.

Interior of the First Doctor's TARDIS

The circles that lined the walls changed. And eventually, when the Eighth Doctor appeared in the 1996 movie, the interior of the TARDIS had changed completely.

The Ninth and Tenth Doctors' TARDIS interiors were bronze-colored with tall, winding pillars, countless tubes hanging from the ceiling, and a central console giving off a strange green glow. The Eleventh Doctor's TARDIS had old-fashioned objects on the control panels, including a typewriter. The Twelfth Doctor changed things up even more with a modern, sleek silver interior.

Interior of the Twelfth Doctor's TARDIS

Doctor Who: The Movie was made for older audiences. It was intended to show viewers what a new season of the show might look like. In the United Kingdom, 9.1 million fans watched this first new televised *Doctor Who* adventure in six years. The Eighth Doctor's first adventure did not have the necessary spark to ignite a new age for the classic program. In the United States, only 5.6 million viewers had tuned in.

After defeating the Master at the end of the movie, the Doctor is once again alone. The future of the character—and the show—did not seem promising.

CHAPTER 6
A New Doctor for a New Age!

For nearly sixteen years there were no new TV episodes of *Doctor Who*. The Doctor's adventures continued in novels, comic books, and radio serials. Reruns were shown every once in a while, but the future of *Doctor Who* did not look bright.

Russell T. Davies

A lifelong fan of the show, writer Russell T. Davies was the man who brought the Time Lord back to television. While many people were doubtful that the show could ever be as great as it once had been, Davies was confident he could make it work.

On March 26, 2005, a man with cropped hair dressed in an old leather jacket ran across television screens in the United Kingdom. He grabbed the hand of a young woman named Rose, saving her from some animated department store mannequins. "Run!" he said. That single word ushered in a new age for *Doctor Who* and for audiences who feared the show had been lost forever.

Instead of following the format of the original show—multiple episodes that were part of a longer story—the new *Doctor Who* would be more like American television shows. Each episode would be longer and tell a story that could stand on its own. The BBC approved a thirteen-episode first season. Unlike older *Doctor Who* episodes, Davies wanted the new Doctor to spend more time on Earth. He believed it would be easier for audiences to enjoy the show if the stories had a more human, and less alien, approach.

Played by Christopher Eccleston, the Ninth Doctor was very different from those who had come before. He had a shaved head, wore simple dark T-shirts and a worn leather jacket, and had a fancy new sonic screwdriver. Gone were the question marks, long scarves, and silly hats— the newly regenerated Ninth Doctor looked dangerous, and for good reason. He was a bit wild. But beneath the wildness, there was anger and sadness. The Doctor was now truly alone in the universe.

Christopher Eccleston as the Ninth Doctor

The stories that Russell T. Davies wrote explained that during the years when he hadn't appeared on television, the Doctor was fighting in the Last Great Time War. This was a violent battle over many years between the Time Lords and the Daleks. The Doctor brought the war to an end by destroying both sides of the conflict. He had stopped the Daleks but had also destroyed his own people. He was the last of the Time Lords, alone in the only remaining TARDIS.

This new *Doctor Who* was an absolute hit. Joined by Rose, Mickey, and Captain Jack Harkness (a fellow time traveler), the Doctor faced off against enemies both new and old. These included store mannequins called Autons, slimy Slitheen, and the return of the Daleks. The first season proved to audiences that *Doctor Who* was back and willing to be bold.

The first episode of the season, "Rose," was viewed by over ten million in the United Kingdom alone. Only four days after it premiered, a second season was announced. A year later, the Sci-Fi Channel released the first season in the United States.

Captain Jack Harkness   Rose   Mickey

By the end of this first season, the Ninth Doctor's attitude had changed. He was no longer alone. He had learned from the humans who had become his new companions. In his final episode, "The Parting of the Ways," the Doctor forces his regeneration in order to save Rose. As he's about to change into the Tenth Doctor, he looks at her and says, "I just want to tell you, you were fantastic. Absolutely fantastic. And you know what? So was I!" And in a blinding flash, a new man appears with wild hair and a charming smile. The Tenth Doctor had been born.

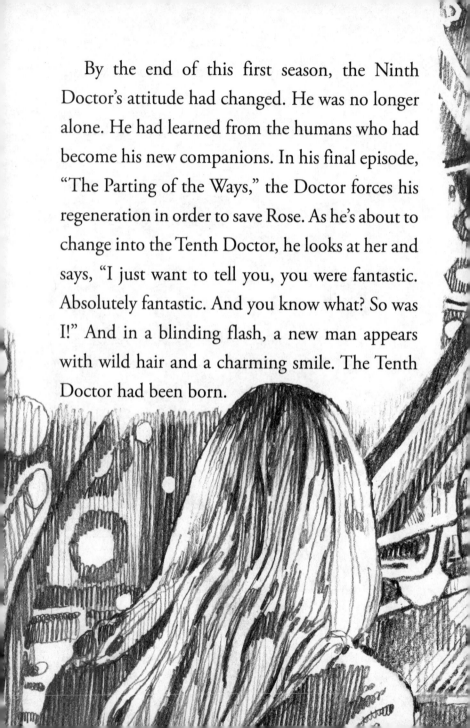

CHAPTER 7
Wibbly-Wobbly Timey-Wimey

"The Christmas Invasion"—which was shown on Christmas Day in 2005—begins with the Doctor recovering from his regeneration. For much of the episode, he's asleep and regaining his strength. Meanwhile, Earth has been invaded by the Sycorax, a dangerous alien race.

When he's needed the most, the Doctor finally wakes up! The episode ends with the Doctor defeating the leader of the Sycorax in a duel. The Sycorax agree to leave Earth behind.

As the ship exits Earth's atmosphere, Prime Minister Harriet Jones, fearful that they will return when the Doctor isn't around, orders that the ship be destroyed. The Doctor is furious! The Sycorax had surrendered. He tells the prime minister she had no right to kill them and that her time as prime minister will come to an end— and it does.

Bigger Budget, Bigger Monsters

When *Doctor Who* first began in 1963, the show had a very limited budget. It was expected to be a fun, educational children's program. The Daleks could be operated only by a person sitting inside each alien body, moving the eye and the weapons with their hands. It was a complex puppet. One of the Daleks' arms was made using a plunger!

By the time the new show appeared in 2005,

Star Whale

the BBC had bigger things planned. *Doctor Who* no longer needed to rely only on effects like costumes, puppets, and models. It used computer-generated imagery (CGI). Soon the Daleks could be made to fly instead of just rolling along.

Gigantic space-traveling whales, towering demons, and other amazing monsters—impossible to create during the '60s and '70s—started to appear on the show regularly.

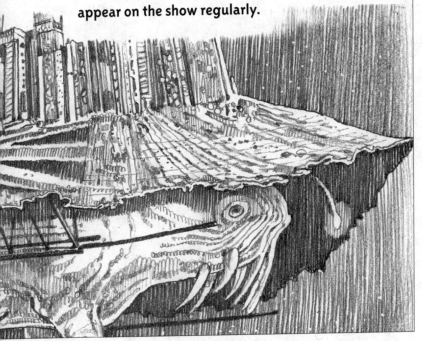

David Tennant as the Tenth Doctor

David Tennant was a huge *Doctor Who* fan before being cast in 2005. Wearing a pair of Converse All Star sneakers, Tennant's Tenth Doctor continued to have adventures with the Ninth Doctor's companion, Rose. He wore tight-fitting brown and blue suits with an overcoat. He was excited by the unknown, fascinated by humans, and became angry when things didn't go the way he expected them to.

Over three seasons and forty-seven episodes, the Tenth Doctor quickly became a fan-favorite. He was often compared to Tom Baker's Fourth Doctor. From 2005 to 2010, the Tenth Doctor tested the limits of time and space.

He meets up with Sarah Jane Smith and K-9 in "School Reunion," becomes human in order to hide from some evil enemies in "Human Nature," and meets his future wife, River Song, in the two-part story "Silence in the Library" and "Forest of the Dead."

The Tenth Doctor with Sarah Jane Smith and K-9

Martha Jones   Donna Noble   Wilfred Mott

Along with a wide assortment of companions—Rose Tyler, Martha Jones, Donna Noble, Wilfred Mott, and Jack Harkness—the Tenth Doctor once again faced many battles. His longtime enemy, the Master, returned, and so did the Cybermen and the Daleks. The Tenth Doctor's adventures brought him face-to-face with water-zombies on Mars, took him aboard the doomed cruise-spaceship *Titanic*, and led him to the planet of the strange alien race the Ood.

While paving the way for two *Doctor Who* spin-off television shows (*Torchwood* and *The Sarah Jane Adventures*), the Tenth Doctor's adventures introduced audiences to one of the most terrifying enemies of all—the Weeping Angels. They are first seen in the stand-alone 2007 episode "Blink." The episode focuses on a young woman named

Scene from "Blink"

Sally Sparrow, and the Doctor appears only briefly. To this day, "Blink" is widely considered to be one of the best episodes of *Doctor Who* ever. It introduced the Doctor's phrase "timey-wimey," used to describe things the Doctor himself cannot really explain.

As 2010 drew to a close, the Tenth Doctor's

time was up. Once again, the Doctor sacrificed himself to save a friend, Wilfred Mott. After being hit with a lethal dose of radiation, the Doctor fights off his regeneration but only for so long. He travels around, observing his companions

at different points in their lives. And as his regeneration draws near, the Doctor returns to his TARDIS. Sensing the end, he looks tearfully ahead and says, "I don't want to go." Fans of the Tenth Doctor didn't want him to go, either.

CHAPTER 8
The Youngest Yet

The Eleventh Doctor first appeared at the end of the Tenth Doctor's final episode. His TARDIS in flames and falling toward Earth, the now much younger Doctor excitedly screamed, "Geronimo!" as he flew out of control toward an uncertain future.

In his first episode, "The Eleventh Hour," the Doctor and the TARDIS crash-land in the backyard of a young girl's house. She witnesses the Doctor, his clothes torn, emerge from the smoking TARDIS. She calls him the "raggedy man" and wants to go with him. He promises to return after fixing his ship. But by the time he

does, the girl has grown into a young woman. She is named Amelia "Amy" Pond. By the end of the first episode, the Doctor has been introduced to her boyfriend, Rory Williams. After defeating an alien threat, the Eleventh Doctor emerges dressed like a professor in a tweed suit coat, suspenders, and a bow tie.

Matt Smith as the Eleventh Doctor and Amy Pond

Although Matt Smith was younger than any actor who had ever played the Doctor, his version of the Doctor was very old and wise. While he himself was only twenty-six at the time, Smith's performance reflected the actual age of the time traveler, who was now over nine hundred years old!

Over the course of three seasons, the Eleventh Doctor became a very complex version of the

Crack in time and space from the fifth season

popular character. His adventures began to reveal his long and complicated past. His journeys with Amy and Rory started like a fairy tale and then became a much longer and larger quest. The fifth season explored the mystery of strange cracks in time and space appearing throughout the universe caused by the future destruction of the TARDIS. River Song returned again and again over three seasons.

The Complicated History of River Song

By far one of the most difficult stories to follow within the show is that of the Doctor's wife, River Song.

In her first appearances in "Silence in the Library" and "Forest of the Dead," she had her own sonic screwdriver and a journal that looked a lot like the TARDIS. At the end of "Forest of the Dead," River revealed to the Doctor that he had given her the sonic screwdriver the last time they'd met. But the Doctor hadn't met River yet!

When River appeared again, meeting the Eleventh Doctor, she recognized him immediately. And, amazingly, she knew how to fly the TARDIS! The story only gets more confusing from there. Eventually, it's revealed that River Song is actually the time-traveling future child of Amy and Rory. Her real name is Melody Pond. Throughout eleven seasons, River pops in and out of the show, always checking her blue notebook to see where in the Doctor's timeline she has arrived.

There's no simple way to explain it, but River Song and the Doctor have a very complicated relationship. Their timelines are going in reverse. The last time River sees the Doctor is the first time he meets her! No matter how confusing it can be, the Doctor always seems to know that River is someone special.

In the sixth season, the Doctor discovers who River Song really is, and he marries her. He then meets the TARDIS in human form for the first

time. The Doctor is introduced to three new unlikely friends—Madame Vastra; her wife, Jenny; and a Sontaran named Strax. Terrifying alien creatures dressed in dark suits called the Silence appear in many of the episodes, erasing the memories of anyone who's seen them.

Vastra, Jenny, and Strax

Midway through the seventh season, the Doctor goes into hiding in Victorian London after the loss of his previous companions. He is protected by his friends Vastra, Jenny, and Strax. While hiding, the Doctor meets a young woman named Clara. The Doctor calls her "the Impossible Girl."

Clara

Clara appears again in modern-day London in the episode called "The Bells of Saint John," and the Doctor decides to take her on as his companion. With a backstory as mysterious as the Doctor's own, Clara comes to play a big role in his past, present, and future. At one point, she jumps into his time stream, chasing after a villain who is attempting to destroy the Doctor once and for all. While being thrown through time and space, Clara meets and saves every version of the Doctor who had come before. She truly was an "Impossible Girl."

Over the course of forty-four episodes, the Eleventh Doctor tangles with old and new enemies—the Silence, the Dream Lord, the Weeping Angels, the Great Intelligence, Daleks, and Cybermen—and has a chance run-in with Adolf Hitler. After all of those terrible threats, the Eleventh Doctor finally dies defending a town called Christmas. After three seasons, Matt Smith decided to leave the show to pursue other acting roles. The character of Clara would remain and meet a very different Doctor in the following season.

An Adventure in Space and Time

This is no ordinary *Doctor Who* episode. The eighty-three-minute-long movie tells the story of the creation of the now classic show. *An Adventure in Space and Time* premiered on the BBC on November 21, 2013.

David Bradley, well known for his role as Argus Filch in the Harry Potter films, was cast as William Hartnell, the actor who played the very first Doctor. For the first time, audiences witnessed the creation of the TARDIS, the building of the Daleks, and the drama that took place behind the scenes of the first few years of the show.

Close to three million viewers tuned in to watch *An Adventure in Space and Time*. David Bradley was so popular as the First Doctor that he returned to play the character again in the 2017 Christmas special "Twice Upon a Time."

David Bradley in *An Adventure in Space and Time*

CHAPTER 9
The One with the Eyebrows

The Twelfth Doctor appeared briefly in *Doctor Who*'s fiftieth-anniversary special, "The Day of the Doctor," in 2013. You might miss him if you blink, because when all the versions of the Doctor came together to prevent the destruction of Gallifrey during the Time War, all that audiences got to see was a glimpse of some very angry eyes and arched gray eyebrows. But it was enough. Fans were more eager than ever to meet the next Doctor.

In the last episode with the Eleventh Doctor, Clara pleaded for him not to change. But where once stood a young, handsome Doctor, a tall, gray-haired man with angry eyebrows appeared. The new Doctor turned to Clara as the TARDIS

spun out of control and asked, "Do you happen to know how to fly this thing?"

The first episode of season eight placed the Doctor once again in Victorian London, where Clara had to be convinced by Vastra, Jenny, and Strax that the new Doctor was really the same man she had known before. After an adventure involving a *Tyrannosaurus rex* and a group of alien cyborgs, Clara is finally convinced. But the

Doctor isn't convinced himself.

Peter Capaldi, a well-known British actor, had been cast as the Twelfth Doctor and was probably more excited than most Whovians at the news! He'd been a fan of the show his entire life, watching it since he was a little boy. He always wanted to be the Doctor, and now he was.

With a dramatic actor like Capaldi on board, the show was able to move in a new direction.

The Twelfth Doctor was curious about his role in the universe. He knew about all the lives and worlds that he had saved, but he wondered if, after all he'd done, he was a good man. Over the course of three seasons, the Doctor struggled with answering this question and many others. Like the professor he eventually became, the new Doctor was thoughtful, curious, and looking for answers.

Peter Capaldi as the Twelfth Doctor

Sunglasses and Guitar

Every regeneration of the Doctor has had a different look. Each costume is an important part of the character. The Twelfth Doctor started out wearing a long black coat, a white shirt, and dark blue pants with black boots. Eventually the pants were replaced with plaid ones and the dress shirt with a T-shirt and hooded sweatshirt. The Doctor began to look like a rock star.

The Twelfth Doctor swapped his sonic screwdriver for a pair of black sunglasses—sonic sunglasses. And he could often be found playing an electric guitar. Sometimes the Twelfth Doctor appeared dressed as a professor and acted like one, too. But when he put on his sunglasses and pulled out his electric guitar, the Twelfth Doctor truly looked like the rebel he was.

While the Eleventh Doctor's seasons focused a lot on the future and things to come, the Twelfth Doctor's time on the show had him looking to the past and trying to fix some of the mistakes he'd made. To make things even more difficult, the Master returns, now regenerated as a woman named Missy! Fearing that his time has come to an end, the Twelfth Doctor returns to his home world of Gallifrey, which was saved during the events of the fiftieth-anniversary special. He wants to make things right.

The Twelfth Doctor finally gets to spend some much-deserved time with his wife, River. He eventually also finds new companions.

They are a university cafeteria worker named Bill
and a cyborg named Nardole.

Nardole and Bill

But soon he would have to regenerate again. In the last moments before his regeneration, the Doctor, so tired of always changing, halts the process and lands on a snowy planet where he is surprisingly met by the very first Doctor.

As the episode "Twice Upon a Time" comes to an end, both Doctors, the first and the last, agree that perhaps it is time to let regeneration happen. They part ways and the Twelfth Doctor returns to his TARDIS, where he finally gives in, saying, "Doctor, I let you go."

He's suddenly surrounded by the light of his regeneration, and when he looks into the reflection of the screen in front of him, a new pair of eyes are staring back. The eyes belong to a woman. The Doctor smiles and utters with joy her first words as the Thirteenth Doctor: "Oh, brilliant."

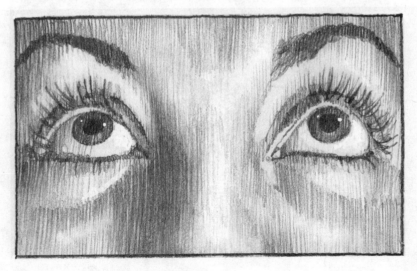

In the fall of 2018, Jodie Whittaker stepped into the shoes of the famous Doctor for her first adventure. A new chapter in the history of the world's favorite time traveler had begun.

Jodie Whittaker as the Thirteenth Doctor

Doctor Who continues to thrill and excite viewers all around the world. Some families have multiple generations who continue to share the magic of the Doctor's travels through time and space together. From movies and television shows to books and more, the world of *Doctor Who* continues to inspire and influence all forms of entertainment, including several spin-off television shows.

The shows *Torchwood*, *The Sarah Jane Adventures*, and *Class* all take place within the world of *Doctor Who*. With over eight hundred episodes and more on the way, *Doctor Who*

continues ever onward through the universe,
thrilling everyone who is waiting to catch another
glimpse of that blue police box.

Bibliography

*Books for young readers

Guerrier, Simon, Steve O'Brien, and Ben Morris. *Doctor Who Whographica: An Infographic Guide to Space and Time.* New York: Harper Design, 2016.

Hearn, Marcus. *Doctor Who: The Vault; Treasures from the First 50 Years.* New York: Harper Design, 2013.

Kistler, Alan. *Doctor Who: A History.* Guilford: Globe Pequot, 2013.

* Loborik, Jason, Neil Corry, Jaqueline Rayner, Andrew Darling, Kerrie Dougherty, David John, and Simon Beecroft. *Doctor Who: The Visual Dictionary: Updated and Expanded.* New York: DK Children, 2014.

Scott, Cavan, and Mark Wright. *Doctor Who: Who-ology.* London: BBC Books, 2013.